A COLONY LEADER

WILLIAM
BRADFORD

BY CHARLES P. GRAVES

ILLUSTRATED BY MARVIN BESUNDER

GARRARD PUBLISHING COMPANY

CHAMPAIGN, ILLINOIS

For my nephew, Michael Weld Minot

Photo on page one courtesy of
The Pilgrim Society
Plymouth, Massachusetts

Contents

1. Orphan Boy

"Put that book down, William," Uncle Robert shouted. "Go watch the sheep!"

"Can't I finish this page?" William begged.

"What book are you reading?" the boy's other uncle, Thomas Bradford, asked.

"The Bible," William replied.

"A ten-year-old boy reading the Bible!" Uncle Robert exclaimed. "I'm sure the bishop would say you are too young to understand it. You should let the minister explain it to you."

"I *can* understand it!" William insisted. "I've as much right to read the Bible as any old bishop."

"Quiet, William!" Uncle Thomas said. "The bishops rule our church, and they know what is right for us."

In those days church officials insisted that only they knew what the Bible meant. They preferred to tell people about the Bible, rather than have people read it themselves. But William was not going to give up his Bible reading.

William Bradford was an orphan. His father, a farmer, had died soon after the boy was born in 1590. His mother died when he was seven.

For three years William had lived with his uncles on a farm near Austerfield, a village in Yorkshire, England. His uncles owned a flock of sheep, and William was their shepherd.

The boy was often lonesome. His uncles tried to be kind to him, but it was not the same as having a mother and father.

William's Bible was a great comfort to him. He especially liked the Bible verse which began:

The Lord is my shepherd;
I shall not want . . .

He often read the Bible during the long hours when he was by himself in the pasture. The boy felt that God was looking after him in the same way he was looking after the sheep.

William's uncles took him to the Church of England every Sunday. All Englishmen were expected to go to the same church and worship God exactly as Queen Elizabeth did. There was an elaborate service full of ceremony which meant little to William. He was disappointed that there was no Bible reading.

He felt that the service and church decorations were too fancy. William knew that decorations such as stained-glass windows, altars, and incense were not mentioned in the Bible. They had all been added since Christ died.

One day William met a boy his own age who felt the same about religion.

"I go to a simple church in Babworth," the boy said. "It's a Puritan church. We want to purify the form of the English church. Our service is centered around the Bible the way services were in olden days."

Babworth was a town nearby. The boy invited William to come to the Puritan church with him.

Early the next Sunday William tiptoed quietly out of the house before his uncles left for their church. Then he walked to Babworth with his friend.

The Puritans met in a farmhouse. Richard Clyfton was their minister. "We can worship God in this farmhouse as well as we could in a cathedral," Clyfton said.

He told the congregation that all men had the right to read the Bible and to decide the meaning for themselves. William was impressed. Clyfton was repeating ideas that were already in William's head.

William's uncles were angry when they learned he had been to a Puritan church. "You will disgrace us," they scolded. "Men have been thrown into prison for criticizing the Queen's church."

But William continued going to Babworth. Richard Clyfton gave wonderful sermons which inspired the boy. There were no sermons in the Austerfield church.

One Sunday William met a wealthy forty-year-old Puritan named William Brewster, a man who was to influence his life. Brewster had been to Cambridge, one of England's great universities, and had lived in London. He had traveled to Holland as a diplomat in the Queen's service. Now he was the postmaster at Scrooby, a town near Austerfield.

Brewster had a large library, and he invited William to use it. William read every chance he got. His uncles realized that he was bright and sent him to school, a privilege in those days. But the village school taught only a few subjects. In Brewster's library William educated himself.

Mr. Brewster became like a father to William, and Mrs. Brewster was kind to him, too. "Make this house your second home," she said.

William and the Brewsters often discussed religious freedom. "The bishops have persecuted many people for refusing to worship as they say," Mr. Brewster told William. "Our church is still officially part of the Church of England, so we've been left alone. But not all Puritans have been so lucky."

"The bishops have no right to tell people how to worship," William protested. "Each congregation should be free to worship as it thinks right."

"I agree," Brewster said with a smile, "but the Queen doesn't. She is head of the Church of England, and she controls the bishops." Then he added thoughtfully, "I'm afraid there will be no real religious freedom in our country while Queen Elizabeth lives."

2. A Great Decision

One spring day in 1603, when William was thirteen, a messenger galloped through Austerfield shouting, "The Queen is dead! Long live the King!"

William's heart skipped a beat when he heard the news. King James of Scotland would now be King of England. Perhaps he would let the people worship as they pleased.

The road that King James took from Scotland to London ran right through Scrooby. William and the Brewsters were in the crowd waiting to see him.

As the King approached, trumpets sounded and drums beat. A troop of horsemen, their lances gleaming in the sun, thundered by in a cloud of dust. William stood on tiptoe and craned his

neck. Then he saw the new King. Dressed in a green coat and a high hat, the new monarch rode slowly by.

The King raised his hand in a royal salute, and a wild cheer arose from the crowd.

"Long live King James!" the people shouted. "God save King James!"

Brewster turned to William and added, "God save religious freedom."

Eight hundred Puritan ministers petitioned King James to reform the church. The King refused.

"Why?" William Bradford asked Brewster when he heard the news.

"That's a good question," Brewster replied. "The King won't admit it, but the real reason is that he's afraid. If he let people decide how to worship, they might want to decide how to govern England. Then the King could lose his job or even his head."

Soon after the King refused the petition, some of the Babworth Puritans decided that they should separate themselves from the Church of England completely. Small groups of reformists, called Separatists, in all parts of England were doing this.

"We can start meeting at my house in

Scrooby," Brewster announced. "But we must meet in secret."

What they were doing was against the law. If they were caught, they might be severely punished.

William was willing to take the risk. Every Sunday he went to church at Scrooby. It made him feel close to God to worship simply.

Several years went by, and William grew tall and sturdy. He worked on his uncles' farm but spent all his spare time with the Brewsters. His uncles did not like this, but they could not keep him from seeing his Scrooby friends.

In 1607, this peaceful way of life came to an end. Spies learned about the group that worshiped at Scrooby. One Separatist was thrown in jail. Some lost their jobs. Brewster and two others were summoned to court. They refused to go and were ordered to pay large fines.

The group met to discuss their future. "Worse punishments lie ahead," Brewster told them. "The jails of London are packed with innocent men who refuse to attend the Church of England."

"Perhaps we should all return to the King's church," a woman said.

"No, never!" cried seventeen-year-old William Bradford. "I'll do anything to be able to worship God as I please."

Brewster looked at the other Separatists. "How many of you feel as William Bradford does?"

Each member of the congregation held up his hand. A smile lit up Brewster's face. He was proud of them.

"There's only one thing to do," he decided. "We must leave England!"

"Where will we go?" William asked.

"To Holland," Brewster replied. "In Holland we can worship as we please. Other Separatists are there now."

"When should we go?"

"As soon as possible," Brewster continued. "But we must go secretly. If King James learns that we plan to leave England, he will try to stop us."

Englishmen had to have permits to leave their country legally. Brewster knew the King would never give permits to the Separatists.

3. Escape to Holland

Brewster hired a ship to take the Separatists to Holland. In great secrecy they slipped away from their homes and went to a port on England's east coast.

One dark spring night they boarded the ship. William stowed his luggage in the hold and climbed back up on deck. Suddenly he heard a loud whistle. A troop of the King's soldiers rushed up to the ship and jumped aboard.

"You are all under arrest!" an officer shouted. Then he saluted the ship's captain. "You have done your job well," the officer said. William's eyes blazed with anger. He knew the captain had betrayed them.

The captives were marched through the streets of the town. The citizens booed and taunted them. "Separatists!" they jeered. "Traitors!"

Along with the others William Bradford was taken to prison. The jail was dirty, and there was never enough to eat. After a month William and most of the others were released.

The Separatists had given up their farms, but they had friends in Scrooby who took them in. William moved back with his uncles.

The next spring the Separatists decided to try again to go to Holland. Brewster hired a Dutch ship and told the captain to meet them at the mouth of a river on a deserted stretch of coast.

The women and children went down the river in a small boat. The men walked.

When they reached the river's mouth, the ship was not there. By the time the ship finally arrived and dropped anchor off shore, it was low tide. The boat carrying the women and children became stuck in the mud. Since it could not be set afloat until high tide, the captain decided to load the men first.

Brewster stayed ashore while William Bradford and some of the other men took a small boat to the ship. Once aboard, William leaned on the rail and watched the boat return to shore for another load.

Suddenly he heard the sound of galloping horses. A large company of armed soldiers had appeared from nowhere and was rapidly approaching the men on shore.

"We must sail at once!" the Dutch captain shouted.

"Leave our wives and children behind!" a man cried. "We can't."

"You must!" the captain bellowed. "We'll all be captured if we stay here." He ordered his crew to hoist the sails and head for Holland.

William felt sorry for the men whose families were left behind. "Brewster will take care of your wives and children," he assured his worried friends. "They can join us later."

Early the next morning William was awakened by the roar of a storm. He could feel the little ship shaking from stem to stern. Climbing up on deck, he was almost blown overboard.

Day after day the storm continued. It seemed as if the ship would be pounded to pieces by the waves. "We are going to sink!" a sailor cried, expressing the fear in everyone's heart.

"Lord," William prayed, "only You can save us."

As if in answer to his prayer, the wind slackened. Soon the sea became calm, and the sun was shining.

A few days later the ship reached Amsterdam.

4. Pilgrims

Several months later Brewster and those who had been left behind escaped to Holland.

William hurried to meet Brewster when he reached Amsterdam. "How do you like it here?" Brewster asked.

"We can worship as we please," William replied, "and I like that. But it is hard to earn a living." Holland didn't need any farmers or clerks, so Bradford had taken a job making cloth. He did not enjoy the work.

After a year in Amsterdam, William and the other members of his church moved to Leyden, a nearby city. They hoped they would find more interesting work there, but jobs were scarce. The Englishmen had to take anything they could get. William again worked making cloth.

Although he didn't earn much money, Bradford was happier now, as he had met a pretty girl named Dorothy May. She was quiet and shy, and Bradford was in love with her. When he was 23 they were married.

Among the Bradfords' friends in Leyden were Alice and Edward Southworth and Elizabeth and Edward Winslow. Winslow was a well-educated man a few years younger than William. He was a printer, and he helped Brewster publish religious books.

Two years after they were married, the Bradfords had a son and named him John. William was proud of the boy and had high hopes for him.

When he was two, John Bradford played with the Southworth children. The English children had many Dutch friends too. By the time the Separatists had been in Holland ten years, their children spoke better Dutch than English.

"I don't like it," Bradford said one night when the Southworths were visiting. "I want my son to grow up as an Englishman."

"There's talk of starting an English colony in America," Alice Southworth said. "It all sounds very exciting."

Her husband frowned. "Live in the wilderness

among wild Indians!" he exclaimed. "That's not for me."

"I'd like it," Bradford said. "I'd like to be my own boss." He still disliked his work. Besides, he missed living in the country.

Several English colonies had been started on the North American continent. All had failed except the one founded at Jamestown, Virginia in 1607.

Captain John Smith, an explorer and founder of Jamestown, had written books about both Virginia and New England. He praised the new land in glowing terms.

Many of the Englishmen in Holland had read his books. William Bradford often discussed them with Brewster. "Our children would have a brighter future in America," he said. "They could own their own farms and businesses there."

William began to dream of living in America.

About this time a group of English Separatists in Amsterdam decided to go there. William was disappointed when he found they were going to settle in Jamestown.

"Jamestown was founded by members of the Church of England," he told Dorothy. "I'm afraid we would have no more religious freedom there than in England."

Most of the Separatists in Leyden felt as William did, so they planned to start a new colony of their own. Among those who decided to go were Bradford, Brewster, and John Carver, a well-to-do merchant and church leader. Brewster and Carver were in their fifties, but they were both strong and healthy.

The men studied maps of America and decided that the mouth of "Hudson's River" would make a good place for a settlement. In the seventeenth century the land there was part of Northern Virginia.

"We will be Pilgrims," William Bradford said, "traveling to a far land so we can build new lives for ourselves and for our children."

The Pilgrims realized that it would cost a lot of money to buy a ship and supplies for the colony. They had some money, but not enough. John Carver went to England in the hope of borrowing more.

He found some London businessmen who would sponsor their expedition. The Pilgrims agreed to send furs, fish, and lumber to England to pay off the loan.

They also obtained permission from King James to settle in America. He did not like the Separatists, but he wanted more colonists in

America to protect his lands from attack by the French and Spaniards. The King would not promise the Pilgrims religious freedom in America, but he agreed not to bother them if they would act peaceably.

Many Separatists in Leyden prepared to go. They they heard some tragic news about their Amsterdam friends who had already sailed for Jamestown.

A violent storm had blown their ship a thousand miles off its course. Most of their food and water had given out, and illness had spread through the ship. By the time it reached Jamestown, only a handful of people were alive.

"That won't happen to us," William grimly promised himself.

But many who had planned to make the trip changed their minds. Even Dorothy decided to leave young John in Holland with her parents. She was afraid he might not survive the long trip to America.

When the businessmen heard how many Pilgrims had decided not to go, they sent for Carver.

"You don't have enough settlers to start a colony," they told him. "We'll have to send some Londoners with you."

The businessmen told the Pilgrims to buy a ship in Holland and sail to England. There a group of settlers from London with another ship would join them. The two ships would sail to America together.

The Pilgrims bought a ship named the *Speedwell*. It was small and not very seaworthy, but it was all they could afford.

Dorothy was crying as they boarded the *Speedwell*. She and William hugged their son and kissed him good-bye.

"We'll send for you, John, as soon as we get settled," William promised. Then he shook hands with Edward and Alice Southworth.

"I wish I were going," Alice said.

"All aboard!" the captain shouted. As the ship inched away from the dock, William stood on deck and waved to his son. Sad as he was to be leaving the boy, he couldn't help being excited. A great adventure lay ahead.

5. The Mayflower

The *Speedwell* sailed into the English port of Southampton and anchored near the *Mayflower,* which was the other ship going to America.

"It looks seaworthy," William told Dorothy. "It must be three times as large as the *Speedwell.*" Actually the *Mayflower* was only a little more than 100 feet long.

William went ashore and met John Carver, who had arrived from London. "The *Mayflower* is crowded," Carver said. "There are about 90 passengers in addition to the crew."

"Are the passengers all Separatists?" William asked.

"Unfortunately not," answered Carver. "Few Separatists wanted to go. Most of the passengers are members of the Church of England. Still, they are a healthy-looking lot and should make good colonists."

William visited the *Mayflower* with Carver. As he stepped aboard, a short, stubby man with red hair approached him and said, "I am Captain Miles Standish. I have been hired to take care of the colony's defense."

Standish took William on a tour of the ship and introduced him to the ship's captain, Christopher Jones. Captain Jones explained that he had been sailing the *Mayflower* for twelve years. "She is a good ship," he said.

It took two weeks to load the ships with supplies. The colonists would need food for the first winter and tools for building houses and plowing land.

Finally in August the two ships set sail for America. The *Speedwell* started leaking badly and returned to an English port for repairs. The *Mayflower* returned with her.

After much work on the *Speedwell* the ships sailed again. Once more the *Speedwell* began leaking, and both ships again returned to England.

"The *Speedwell* doesn't speed very well," William Bradford said with a grin. "I think we should abandon it."

"I agree with you," said John Carver.

The Pilgrim leaders decided that everyone should sail on the *Mayflower*.

"We must hurry and move our supplies from the *Speedwell*," Carver said. "We must reach America before winter. We've already lost precious time."

"Let's go back to Holland," Dorothy Bradford pleaded with her husband. She missed little John and was worried about him.

"No," William insisted. "The *Mayflower* will be terribly crowded, but we can stand it for a few weeks."

Some of the passengers decided not to make the trip or to travel on a later ship. So on September 6, 1620, the *Mayflower* sailed again with 102 passengers and a crew of about 30.

Dorothy gazed wistfully at the shore disappearing rapidly in the distance. She was dismayed when she saw their living quarters. Most of the passengers lived together in one large area below the main deck. The Bradfords had only a few square feet of space to themselves. Here William stored their belongings and put down the uncomfortable straw mats on which they slept.

There was no way to bathe and little to eat except dried fish, hardtack, and cheese. The passengers were wet and cold much of the time, and many of them were seasick, including Dorothy. "I've never been so miserable in my life," she complained.

But not William Bradford. "With God's help it will all be over soon," he said. "And think what our reward will be! New homes in a New World where we can worship as we please. A few uncomfortable weeks is a small price to pay for that."

Dorothy felt even worse when a storm lashed out of the west and struck the *Mayflower* in all its fury. Mountainous waves battered the deck, and icy water seeped down on the passengers huddled below.

At the height of the storm, as William stepped on deck to see the captain, he heard a terrified scream. A man named John Howland had fallen overboard.

William rushed to the rail. Some ropes from the masts were trailing in the water.

"Grab a rope!" he yelled.

Howland grabbed a rope and hung on with all his might. Two seamen quickly lowered a long pole, called a boat hook, and fished Howland out of the sea.

The ship tossed and shook. Suddenly William heard a noise that sounded like an explosion.

Captain Jones discovered that one of the ship's main beams had cracked.

William and the other Pilgrim leaders met with Captain Jones and some of the crew to examine the beam.

"We are in deadly peril," a seaman cried. "The ship might break in two."

"Let's turn back," another crewman said.

"Turn back!" William exclaimed. "It's too late now. We have no homes to return to!"

To William's relief, Captain Jones believed the ship could be repaired. When the wind died down and the sea became calm, the ship's carpenter managed to fix the beam.

"There's no doubt in my mind that God is watching over us," William told Dorothy as the *Mayflower* sailed on.

Finally, after two months at sea, Captain Jones told the passengers he thought they were nearing land. On the sixty-sixth day of the voyage, William got up early and climbed on deck.

Suddenly, from the crow's nest, the lookout cried, "Land ahoy!"

William's eager eyes searched the horizon. He saw a dark, thin line ahead, and his heart pounded with excitement. "America at last!" he shouted.

6. Cape Cod

William went to see Captain Jones. "Where are we?" he asked.

"We are nearing Cape Cod," the Captain said. "It's part of the land that Captain John Smith named New England."

"How far is Hudson's River from here?"

"I'm not sure," Captain Jones said, "but we should reach it in several days." He set the ship on a course to the south.

But the *Mayflower* soon ran into angry, shallow water. There were dangerous reefs and shoals everywhere, and the waves boiled over them. Captain Jones was afraid the ship would be wrecked if he continued on his present course. He called the male passengers into his cabin for a meeting.

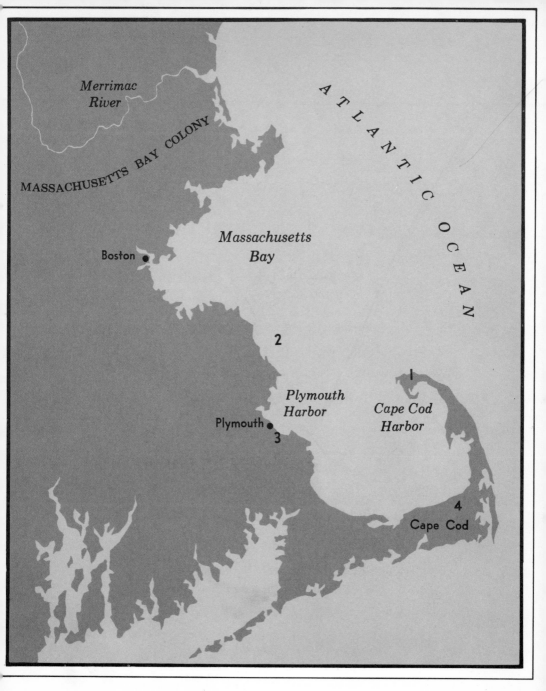

1. Present-day Provincetown, where Bradford and a
   group of Pilgrims first landed in America.

2. The coastal waters of New England, which Bradford
   explored while seeking a site for the new colony.

3. Plymouth, the colony founded by the Pilgrims.
   William Bradford became its first governor.

4. Cape Cod, where Bradford led a party of Pilgrims
   in search of food.

"To reach Hudson's River safely," he began, "we must sail back out to sea and circle south, avoiding the shoals. That might take two weeks or more. Winter is almost here. Perhaps it would be better if you settled in New England."

"I think we should stay here," said John Carver.

"I think so, too," William Bradford agreed.

"We don't have permission to settle in New England," Edward Winslow protested.

"We can settle in New England first," William said, "and get permission later."

The men decided to remain in New England, if they could find a good place to build a settlement. The ship headed back toward the tip of Cape Cod. Captain Jones' maps showed a good harbor on the far side.

Early on the morning of November 11, 1620, the *Mayflower* rounded the Cape. John Carver called the men together for another meeting.

"We must make plans for our government before we go ashore," he said.

Bradford and Brewster helped Carver write a plan. It said that the men would join together in a "civil body." The civil body would make just and equal laws for the good of the colony. All the settlers had to promise to obey the laws.

"Nothing like this could be written in England," Carver observed. "The King wants to make all the laws himself."

William signed the paper gladly. This paper is known today as the *Mayflower Compact*. While it was not true democracy as we know it today, it was the beginning of government by the people.

After the compact was signed, the men elected John Carver as their first governor. "Now we must find a place to build our town," Governor Carver announced.

"It must have a good harbor," Brewster said, "where ocean-going ships can anchor."

"It must have pure water for drinking," Winslow added.

"And it must have open fields where we can plant crops next spring," suggested Bradford.

"It should also be easy to defend," Miles Standish declared. "We don't know whether the Indians will be friendly."

The *Mayflower's* anchor soon splashed into the calm waters of Cape Cod Harbor, now called Provincetown Harbor. William Bradford stood on deck and gazed at the sandy shore. It looked bleak, desolate, and utterly deserted. He wondered what unknown dangers lurked there.

7. Indians!

William Bradford and some of the other Pilgrims rowed ashore in the *Mayflower's* long-boat. As soon as they reached the beach, they fell on their knees. "Thank you, Oh Lord," Bradford prayed, "for bringing us safely over the vast and furious ocean."

The Pilgrims started through the woods, hoping to find fresh water. Finding none, they decided that this was not a good place to settle.

A small sailing vessel, called a shallop, had been brought on the *Mayflower*. The Pilgrims planned to use it for fishing.

"Let's explore in the shallop," Bradford suggested. "We can cover more territory that way."

But the shallop had been damaged on the voyage. It would take several days to repair it.

"We can't wait," Bradford said. "We must find a place to settle before the ground is covered with snow."

Governor Carver ordered Miles Standish to take some men exploring. "It may be a dangerous trip," Standish said. "Who will volunteer?"

"I will," Bradford said, stepping forward. Several other men joined him.

"Put on your armor," Standish told the men, "and bring your muskets and swords."

The explorers started down the beach. When they had gone a short distance, Bradford saw a group of figures ahead.

"Indians!" he cried. "Look!"

At the same moment the Indians saw the Pilgrims. Whooping wildly, they fled into the woods.

"Let's go after them," Bradford said. "If we can become friendly with the Indians, they might help us find a place to settle."

The Pilgrims tried to catch up with the Indians, but they couldn't move fast enough in their heavy armor.

After several days the Pilgrims returned to the *Mayflower,* having found no place to settle. The shallop was repaired, however, and Bradford went on another exploration trip. This too failed.

Bradford talked to Robert Coppin, one of the mates on the *Mayflower.* "You have been to New England before," Bradford said. "Have you any idea where we might settle?"

"I'm not sure," Coppin replied, "but I know there is a good harbor just across the bay. We named it 'Thievish Harbor' because the Indians there stole a harpoon from us. On Captain John Smith's map, it is called Plymouth."

"Can you take us there in the shallop?" Bradford asked.

"I'll try," Coppin agreed.

When Bradford said good-bye to Dorothy, she begged him not to go. "Indians may kill you."

"I must go," Bradford insisted. "Most of the other men are sick."

So Bradford, Coppin, Standish, and a few other men sailed along the coast in the shallop. Each night they went ashore to sleep.

One night they were awakened by wild howls and roars. "Arm! Arm!" a sentry shouted. The men grabbed their muskets and rushed out into the darkness. The howling stopped.

"I think it must have been wolves," Coppin said.

The next morning, as they ate breakfast, the howling started again.

"Indians!" a sentry shouted. "They're all around us!"

Most of the men had already put their muskets in the shallop, but Standish and Bradford still had theirs. A curtain of arrows fell around them as they shot at the Indians. The other men soon got their muskets and joined the fight.

Some of the Indians fled, but one brave warrior stood behind a tree and fired arrow after arrow at the Pilgrims. Standish took careful aim at the tree. His shot made the bark explode about the Indian's ears.

The Indian shrieked with terror and ran. The other Indians followed, and the fight was over.

8. Plymouth

Bradford and the other volunteers boarded the shallop and continued their voyage. It began to rain, and soon the rain turned to snow. The men were soaked and shivering.

The wind whipped the sea into such heavy waves that the shallop's rudder broke. Two men steered with an oar. It was hard work.

"Do you know where we are?" Bradford asked Coppin.

"I think that's Plymouth Harbor ahead," Coppin answered, pointing to an opening between two points of land. "We must try to reach the harbor while we can still see." As it was getting dark, Coppin ran up more sail on the shallop's mast so it would go faster. In a sudden gust of wind the mast bent.

"Lower the sail!" Bradford shouted.

It was too late. With a thunderous crack the mast broke into three pieces and fell overboard with the sail.

"Grab the oars and start rowing!" Coppin yelled. Bradford grabbed an oar as the wind and the tide swept the little vessel toward shore. Giant breakers were crashing on the beach. It looked as if the shallop would be wrecked.

"Row as you've never rowed before!" Bradford commanded.

The men pulled on the oars with all their might. Finally, they succeeded in steering the shallop into the lea of a small island that separated Plymouth Harbor from the open sea.

The Pilgrims went ashore and built a fire. They were wet and cold. "Thank God we are safe," Bradford whispered.

The next day was clear, and the men rested and dried their clothes. The following day they boarded the shallop again and measured the depth of the harbor. They found it was deep enough to float the *Mayflower* and other ocean-going vessels. Rowing to the mainland, they landed at the place marked "Plymouth" on Captain Smith's map.

Bradford was pleased when they found several brooks with pure, sparkling water. Nearby they discovered cornfields that had not been used in recent years.

"It will be easy to plant crops here," Bradford pointed out, "but where are the Indians who cleared this land?"

"That's a mystery," Coppin said. "I saw them when I was here before."

"Perhaps the Indians have moved away," a Pilgrim suggested.

Bradford felt their search was at an end. "This is a good place for our settlement," he said. "Let's row back to the *Mayflower* and bring it here." He was exhausted but happy.

His happiness did not last long. When Bradford reached the ship, terrible news awaited him. Dorothy was dead. She had fallen overboard and drowned. No one had seen her fall nor heard her cries for help.

Bradford, overcome with grief, fought back the tears. "Work is the best cure for sorrow," he told himself. "And there's plenty of work to be done at Plymouth."

9. Governor Bradford

Bradford stood on deck as the *Mayflower* sailed into Plymouth Harbor on December sixteenth. He shut his eyes and imagined what Plymouth would look like in a few years. He could see a prosperous settlement with happy, God-fearing people.

"A lot of work has to be done before my dream comes true," Bradford realized.

The Pilgrims lived on the ship and went ashore each day, except Sunday, to work. The first thing they built was a storehouse for supplies. Bradford had never worked so hard in his life. He chopped down trees, sawed wood, and gathered thatch for the storehouse roof.

While working he always kept a sharp eye for Indians. Every now and then an Indian or two would appear at the edge of the woods, but when the Pilgrims approached them, the Indians ran away.

The storehouse was finished, and work on other houses began. While they labored the Pilgrims were cold, wet, and half-starved. Many became sick, and the storehouse was turned into a hospital.

William Bradford and Governor Carver were among those ill. They were moved to bunks in the storehouse. One night Bradford smelled smoke.

He saw that a spark from a campfire had ignited the thatched roof. "Let's get out of here!" he shouted. He and the other sick men leaped from their beds and ran outside. Filling buckets of water from the brook, they put out the fire.

Bradford got better, but Carver was desperately ill. Every few days one or more of the settlers died. Eighteen wives had come over on the *Mayflower,* but only five were still alive at the end of the winter. Many children were now orphans, and Bradford helped take care of them.

In spite of the hardships and tragedy, none of the Pilgrims thought of returning to Europe. Members of their faith were still being persecuted in England. Here in Plymouth they could worship as they saw fit. Each Sunday, they held services aboard ship or in the storehouse. Their surroundings were simple, but their hearts were full of joy. "At last we can practice our faith freely and still be Englishmen," they said.

The Londoners wanted to remain in Plymouth too. Here in the New World they could own land. Few people could hope to own land in England.

March came and with it better weather. One day a tall Indian warrior stepped out of the forest and walked calmly into the settlement.

"Welcome!" the Indian said. "My name is Samoset."

The Pilgrims were so astonished they could hardly speak. Finally Bradford asked, "Where did you learn English?"

"I come from the North," Samoset explained in broken English. "English fishermen there taught me their language."

Bradford nodded. He knew that Englishmen had been fishing off the coast for many years, and they often traded with the Indians.

Samoset cleared up the mystery of the empty Indian cornfields. He told the Pilgrims that the Patuxet Indians, who formerly lived at Plymouth, had been wiped out by a terrible disease.

"There is only one Patuxet left," Samoset went on. "His name is Squanto. Squanto was kidnaped by sailors and taken to England. While he was there, the disease struck his tribe. Recently, a kind sea captain brought Squanto back here."

"Bring Squanto to see us," William told Samoset. William realized that Squanto, with his knowledge of the land around Plymouth, might be able to help the settlers.

A week later Samoset returned. "Squanto has been living with the Wampanoag Indians, a two-day march from here," he said. "He is on his way here now with the Wampanoag chief, Massasoit."

"We must do our best to make our visitors welcome," Bradford told the other Pilgrim leaders.

"And to impress them," Captain Standish said, "with the strength of our settlement."

Before long, Massasoit arrived with Squanto and 20 warriors. Dressed in their finest clothes, Bradford and Captain Standish led the Indians to a half-finished house which they had furnished with a green rug and cushions. Then Governor Carver arrived, followed by men beating drums and sounding trumpets.

The Pilgrims and Indians sat on the rug and

exchanged gifts. With Squanto's help as translator, they made a treaty. The Pilgrims and the Wampanoags agreed to help each other in case either were attacked by another Indian tribe. More important, they agreed never to attack each other.

"This is the best thing that could happen to Plymouth," Bradford said to Captain Jones.

"And now that you're safe I must sail back to England," Jones said.

Bradford gave Captain Jones a letter addressed to Edward and Alice Southworth. In it he told them the sad news of Dorothy's death. Then the group said good-bye to the Captain and wished him Godspeed.

Shortly after the *Mayflower* sailed, Governor Carver died. The Pilgrims met to elect a new governor.

"I nominate William Bradford," Brewster said. "I've known him since he was a boy. There's not a better man here."

The others agreed with Brewster. Now William Bradford, aged 31, became Governor Bradford.

10. The First Thanksgiving

Samoset and Massasoit left Plymouth after the treaty was signed, but Squanto remained behind. He went to see Bradford.

"I am accustomed to English ways," he told Bradford. "And this used to be my home. May I live here?"

Bradford was delighted. He knew that Squanto would be invaluable to the Pilgrims in their dealings with the Indians. Squanto also proved helpful in other ways.

"Governor," he told Bradford one warm spring day, "it is time to plant corn. I will show you how."

Corn was native to America and was grown by the Indians. The Pilgrims had never planted it before.

"First, we must catch some fish," Squanto told Bradford. "Get a bucket and come with me."

The brook was alive with fish and, in a short time, Squanto had a bucketful. He and Bradford went to the field where the men were plowing.

Squanto picked up a hoe and raked the earth into a small hill. Then he buried three fish in the hill. "The fish will make the corn grow higher and faster," he explained.

Most of the Pilgrims were city folk and knew little about farming, hunting, or fishing. Squanto helped them dig clams and catch lobsters. He showed the children which berries and nuts were good to eat, and where to find wild salad greens. Without his help the Pilgrims might have starved.

Bradford was one of the few Pilgrims who had farming experience. He showed the men how to plant English vegetables. "How wonderful to feel the soil in my hands again," he exclaimed.

The Governor waited anxiously for the crops to ripen. Would there be enough food to last through the coming winter? The English vegetables did not do well, but the Indian corn was a great success. At last everyone had enough to eat.

"Squanto," Bradford said, "we have you to

thank for our success, you and our Christian God."

Bradford often talked to Squanto about Christianity. He hoped to convert him, and later, the other Indians who lived near Plymouth.

To celebrate the good harvest, Bradford decided to have a festival of thanksgiving. He called the men together.

"Captain Standish, take some men and shoot as many ducks and geese as you can. Squanto will go and invite Chief Massasoit to a feast."

Standish and his hunters had wonderful luck. They returned with enough geese and ducks to feed a small army. The women started cooking the game. Bradford had long tables set up outdoors.

The next day Massasoit arrived with 90 hungry warriors. Bradford was afraid there might not be enough food to feed them all, but Massasoit sent his braves out to hunt. They returned with five deer.

For three days the celebration went on. The

men had shooting contests, and the children played games. Everyone had a wonderful time. This festival was the first American Thanksgiving.

As Governor Bradford watched the happy Pilgrims, he couldn't help thinking how much happier he would be if he had a family. He thought of Dorothy, who had drowned, and of his son John, who had stayed in Holland.

"But I'm alive," Bradford said to himself, "and I believe Plymouth will live." He looked around at the row of houses ready for the winter and at the fort being built on a nearby hill. "We have a great deal to be thankful for," he said.

11. A New Family

Shortly after Thanksgiving an Indian messenger raced into Plymouth. He told Squanto that there was a strange ship off Cape Cod, headed straight for Plymouth. Squanto ran to the Governor's house with the news.

"Is it an English ship?" Bradford asked excitedly. "Or French? Or a pirate ship?"

"The messenger doesn't know," Squanto said. "He can't tell one flag from another."

"Captain Standish," Bradford called. "Get ready to defend Plymouth."

Standish ordered all the men in his little army to prepare to fight. They shouldered their muskets and marched down to the shore. But when the ship sailed into the harbor, the Pilgrims saw the English flag flying from her mast. The ship was the *Fortune*. It brought welcome news. The Pilgrims had official permission to settle in Plymouth.

The ship also brought 35 new settlers. Bradford was concerned when he learned that they had no food or supplies with them.

"We have hardly enough food for ourselves," he said. But there was nothing he could do except welcome the new settlers.

A few days after the ship left, a fierce Indian warrior stalked into Plymouth. His tribe, the Narragansetts who lived to the south, were enemies of the Pilgrims' friends, the Wampanoags.

When the warrior reached Governor Bradford's house, he flung down a bundle of arrows tied with a snakeskin.

The Governor called Squanto. "What does this mean?" he asked.

"It is a challenge," Squanto explained. "It is the Indian way of declaring war. The Narragansetts hope you will go away so they can conquer the Wampanoags and rule this land."

"What should we do?" Bradford asked.

"Guns are more deadly than arrows," Squanto replied. "Indians are afraid of guns. I suggest that you return the snakeskin to the Narragansetts stuffed with musket balls."

So Governor Bradford filled the snakeskin with ammunition and sent it back to the Narragansetts. The Indians were frightened and did not attack.

The next spring William Bradford was re-elected governor. The Pilgrims liked him and knew that he was an able leader.

More ships with more settlers began coming to Plymouth. Slowly the colony grew. In the summer of 1622, a ship brought Bradford a letter from Alice Southworth. She told him that her husband, like Dorothy Bradford, had died suddenly.

"That means Alice is free to marry again," Bradford thought. "Perhaps she will come to Plymouth and be my wife."

When the ship left, it carried a letter from the Governor asking Alice to marry him. Despite the hard life the Pilgrims led, he felt sure she and her children would like New England.

Winter was approaching again, and now the Governor was worried. Would there be enough food for all the new settlers?

With Squanto and some other men, Governor Bradford went on a trading expedition to Cape Cod. He hoped to buy corn and beans from the Indians there.

The expedition was successful in obtaining food,

but Squanto became ill. Bradford tried to cure him, but Squanto grew worse and worse.

Squanto realized that he was going to die. He took Bradford's hand and said, "Pray for me, Governor. I want to go to the English God, in Heaven."

When Bradford returned to Plymouth after Squanto's death, his sorrow was tempered by some good news. There was a letter from Alice telling him that she would be happy to be his wife. Bradford read her letter over and over again. Now he would have a family of his own! Alice arrived the following year on the *Ann*—alone.

"Where are your children?" Bradford asked as she came ashore.

"I left them behind," Alice said. "They will come later."

A few years after Alice and William Bradford were married, Alice's two children came to Plymouth. So did Bradford's son John, now twelve years old.

The Bradford house was a noisy, lively place. It was small but comfortable with two rooms downstairs. The children slept in the attic.

As the years went by, Alice and William had three children of their own. There were many children in Plymouth now, and they led busy lives. As they grew up they learned to hunt and fish. John Bradford was the envy of the younger boys when his father took him to an Indian village where they traded cloth and knives for beaver pelts.

"The pelts will be shipped to England where they will bring high prices," Bradford told his son.

Alice Bradford taught the girls to bake cornbread in the big fireplace and to make candles and soap. Bradford taught the boys how to farm. There were many fields outside Plymouth now, and recent ships had brought cows, sheep, pigs, and chickens.

On winter evenings the children studied around the fireplace with their father. "I want you to be able to read the Bible yourselves," he said.

Sunday was observed strictly. Early in the morning the Bradfords and their friends marched up the hill to the fort where services were now held.

They had no minister at first, so William Brewster, as the oldest man in the colony, preached the sermon. The service often lasted three hours. There was another long service in the afternoon.

The Pilgrims insisted that everyone—Puritans and Church of England members alike—keep Sunday strictly as they did. No work or play of any kind was allowed. The Bradford children were always glad when Sunday was over.

Although the Pilgrims had left England to worship as they pleased, there was little religious freedom in Plymouth.

12. Pilgrim's Pride

As the years went by, more and more settlements were started in New England. The Massachusetts Bay Colony was founded north of Plymouth. In 1630, 1,000 Puritans arrived from England and built the town of Boston.

"A thousand settlers!" Governor Bradford exclaimed when he heard the news. "That's three times as many as have come to Plymouth in ten years."

"Maybe Boston is bigger than Plymouth," Alice said. "But we were here first. New England history begins with Plymouth."

Bradford was thoughtful for a moment. "That gives me an idea," he said. "I'm going to write the history of Plymouth, so our children and their children will know how Plymouth was founded."

Bradford called his history *Of Plymouth Plantation*. In it he told how the Separatists had escaped from England to Holland and how they had come to America on the *Mayflower* and settled Plymouth. Each year, he added to the history.

Except for five years, Bradford was Governor of Plymouth for the rest of his long life. The people had confidence in him and kept re-electing him. He was proud that he could serve them so faithfully.

As Bradford grew older he saw other New England colonies growing and prospering. But the soil around Plymouth was not very fertile. Many people in Plymouth were moving away.

"Plymouth has fewer people now," the colony leader said, "than it had in 1623. It is like an ancient mother grown old and forsaken by her children." However, the "children" carried the spirit of Plymouth far and wide.

If Plymouth was a mother, as Bradford said, then he was certainly the colony's father. His courage and hard work had kept Plymouth alive in the early years.

William Bradford died in 1657. That was more than 300 years ago. But it is Bradford and the other founders of Plymouth whom Americans honor when they sing:

Land of the Pilgrim's pride
From every mountain side
Let Freedom ring!